Tell It Slant

by
Maev Mac Coille

Published by Playdead Press 2020

© Maev Mac Coille 2020

Maev Mac Coille has asserted her rights under the Copyright, Design and Patents Act, 1988, to be identified as the author of this work.

A CIP catalogue record for this book is available from the British Library.

ISBN 978-1-910067-87-1

Caution
All rights whatsoever in this play are strictly reserved and application for performance should be sought through the author before rehearsals begin. No performance may be given unless a license has been obtained.

This book is sold subject to the condition that it shall not by way of trade or otherwise, be lent, resold, hired out, or otherwise circulated without the publisher's prior consent in any form of binding or cover other than that in which it is published and without a similar condition including this condition being imposed on the subsequent purchaser.

Playdead Press
www.playdeadpress.com

Maev Mac Coille

Maev was born in Belfast and grew up in Dublin. She studied English Literature and History at Trinity College Dublin, and Theatre and Playwriting at Royal Holloway, University of London.

Writing for theatre includes: *Pain Management, A Raisin, I Think You're Amazing* (Theatre503); *A Poison Tree* and *The Broken* (Arcola/Miniaturists); *Project A* (Camden People's Theatre); *A Door* (LiT Space, London, and Courtyard Theatre, Brisbane); *Modest Stillness and Humility* and *The Woman Who* (Dogstar); *Towards a Standard Drop* (Hackney Showrooms); *The Monsterhouse* (Criterion New Writers showcase); *The Broken Whale* (Peacock Theatre, Dublin); *No Coughing* (A gala event at Abbey Theatre, Dublin); *Simple Procedures* (Etcetera Theatre); *The Optimists* (The White Bear); *The Saddest Lines* and *Mirror, Mirror* (Ramjam Records for Merry Spinsters Theatre Company).

Maev is a graduate of the Abbey Theatre's New Playwrights Programme and the Criterion New Writing Programme. Maev won the St Andrew's Young Playwright of the Year Award in 2001. She has been longlisted for the Papatango, Verity Bargate and Bread and Roses playwriting awards, and nominated for the Susan Smith Blackburn Prize. *Tell It Slant* is her first full-length stage play.

With Thanks To

Erica Miller for bringing *Tell It Slant* to the stage, Ruth McGowan at Dublin Fringe Festival and Melissa Dunne of Papercut Theatre for their support and guidance throughout the production, Catie Dargue, Sandra Rafter, Henry Martin, Laura Hynes, Jenny Mac A Bháird, my extended family and everyone who supported the production. Special thanks to the cast, and everyone at the Hope Theatre and PlayDead Press.

Tell It Slant was first performed at the Hope Theatre, London, on 25 February 2020. The cast was as follows:

DARA/VICK	**Joshua Jewkes**
DARA/VICK	**Clíodhna McCorley**
ALEX	**Vincent Shiels**
SAM	**Alia Sohail**

DIRECTOR	**Erica Miller**
WRITER	**Maev Mac Coille**
DESIGNER	**Constance Villemot**
LIGHTING DESIGNER	**Toby Smith**
SOUND DESIGNER	**Frank David of Audio Jigsaw**

For my parents, without whom *Tell It Slant* would not have come to be, and for Aerin, who never got to see it.

CHARACTERS:

DARA

VICK

SAM

ALEX | *more senior, so noticeably older than the others*

NICK | *present only as a voice*

The characters can be played by actors of any sex.

The company should consist of two male and two female actors.

If possible, the company should be able to swap roles throughout the run, so that Dara and Vick can be played by as a same-sex or opposite sex couple.

If playing as an opposite sex couple, the two actors should swap roles each night, playing opposite sides of the dynamic.

A NOTE ON DIALOGUE:

A – at the end of the line signifies an interruption.

A / signifies overlapping dialogue.

SCENE ONE

A press office. It should feel like a bunker, though it doesn't have to resemble one. Nothing should be neat or shiny. (If possible, there should be a large tv screen, muted, broadcasting a 24 hour news channel, which will begin to reflect the action on stage. However, this is not essential).

As time progresses, the press office should feel as though the walls are closing in – as the pressure on the characters grows, the space becomes more oppressive, sound bouncing around with no escape possible.

The day's papers should be visible. None of them have been touched.

Sam enters with a cup of tea in one hand, and a mobile phone in the other. Sam sits, relaxes, and continues to review the weekend's press on the phone. It is an entertaining read.

Finished laughing, Sam stands, quickly sorts through the papers, and sets one aside.

Dara enters, also looking at a phone.

DARA: I don't want to talk about cats.

SAM: Sorry?

DARA: Ever. Again.

SAM: But you're so very, very good at it.

DARA: Shut up

SAM: (*Beat*) So, busy weekend?

DARA: Oh, it started fine. There were three blissful hours when the phone didn't even ring. I took a whole bath.

SAM: Was it a really good bath?

DARA: There isn't a good enough bath in the world, Sam.

SAM: Depends who else is in the bath with you, doesn't it?

DARA: How many – how many times have we asked them *not* to send out the Freedom of Information requests at a minute to six on Friday evening? I swear I have that with them conversation every three months, and still their itchy fingers can't resist hitting the send button.

SAM: (*Mocking*) You do know freedom of information requests are critical in allowing the public to hold us to account?

DARA: And transparency is a key public virtue and it's like we've been indoctrinated by them. (*Beat*) I'm not saying don't send – we have to send – I'm saying, don't send at a minute to six on a Friday evening. And you cannot convince me that our pest control problem is worthy of two full days of press coverage.

SAM: Technically it was thirty–six hours.

DARA: Whatever.

SAM: It's August

DARA: I *hate* August. Every year, every year it's like this. And what do they want us to do, wait until the vermin are literally running across our desks before doing anything?

SAM: I think they want us to have been competent enough never to have had a vermin problem to begin with, which, not going gonna lie, kind of on their side on that one.

DARA: And those animal charity... *people* owe –

SAM: People?

DARA: I can't think of a word that's office appropriate and conveys the full length and depth and breadth of my bitterness, so... They owe me a massage and some time in an isolation tank, after the weekend they just put me through. Did you see the online poll they did?

SAM: Yeah, I voted in it.

DARA: You voted – thank you, that was helpful.

SAM: I didn't mean it to be helpful, I just like cats.

DARA: I like cats! I never want to see one again after this weekend, but they were extremely cute, even if I wanted to destroy them when I saw their faces on the front page yesterday morning.

SAM: You wanted to kill the cats?

DARA: I wanted to kill something. I don't think you're focusing on my point here.

SAM: You have one? I thought you just wanted to complain.

DARA: I can do both. (*Beat*) I liked the ginger, but anyway. That doesn't make it less annoying.

SAM: Well of course *you* liked the ginger.

DARA: Of course?

SAM: She was outvoted three to one.

DARA: So? She was still cute.

SAM: And yet unloved by the cruel world.

DARA: Thank you. (*Beat*) One of them said the most amazing thing to me.

SAM: Yeah?

DARA: It was after I'd put the line out on twitter, on the second day.

SAM: Now *that* was amazing.

DARA: Too much?

SAM: The loving care and attention that all pets deserve?

DARA: The phones were blowing up, I had to do something, and we weren't turning down a generic cat any more, we were refusing a home to one of two adorable cats selected by the public in their infinite wisdom to guard our building against the scourge of mice. We had to sound like we weren't heartless, though I'd argue the survival of the fittest style poll wasn't exactly loving, not when you really think about it. This cat gets a home and this cat gets...well who cares. Anyway, I was trying to gently point out to that idiot from the Metro that there are places round here that you don't want a cat wandering into – imagine if it got stuck, or poisoned, or –

SAM: And?

DARA: And he said "well, have you tried telling the cat it's not allowed to go there?" (*Beat*) I didn't know where to start.

SAM: Did you laugh?

DARA: No. Well, not on the phone. Afterwards, yes.

SAM: Not met many cats, has he?

DARA: His powers of observation are pretty limited, so I wouldn't assume. He's the one who only noticed he and Alex have the same first name on their fifth email exchange – he's the worst investigative journalist in the world.

SAM: Worse than the ones who make stuff up and hack phones and –

DARA: At least they're competent. (*Beat*) It might not be the stupidest thing I've ever heard from a journalist, but it's got to be up there.

SAM: I keep saying we should have a wall of fame.

DARA: It would only get FOIed. (*Beat*) The rest of it wasn't so bad.

SAM: Yeah, other than the cats, it's really pretty light. Slow news days.

DARA: First news story of my career that made it to the front page, and it *had* to be –

SAM: I saved it for you.

Sam hands Dara the paper

DARA: (*Annoyed*) Thank you. By two o'clock yesterday I was so tired I was praying for something, anything, to happen so the phone would stop ringing, I didn't even care what. And every time it did ring it was Caimin Finlay. It got to the point I was flinching whenever his number came up.

SAM: I'm surprised it's taken you this long to develop that reaction.

DARA: Why can't national treasures pass away at a great age, in their sleep, when it would be *useful*?

SAM: Silly season and the great news desert of August will be over soon, so you can stop wishing death on the great and the good.

DARA: Because we will no longer be interesting.

SAM: More to the point, we'll be fully staffed again.

DARA: *Oh.*

SAM: Forgot about that, did you?

DARA: That's today. Great.

SAM: Try not to frighten this one away.

DARA: It's really *not* my fault – hacks take the job thinking it'll be a nice quiet life, and then run screaming when they realise how much actual work they have to do.

SAM: We've been short staffed for three months now, and it would be really nice not to be. So try not to be antagonising, even if you aren't looking forward to meeting your number one fan.

DARA: That is a gross exaggeration –

SAM: It really isn't.

DARA: A few occasionally pleasant conversations don't mean –

SAM: Not one of them likes *me* that much.

DARA: Yes, but that's because I'm nicer than you.

SAM: Oh, I'm nice. You flirt.

DARA: I do not. And if I do, it's not on purpose, you can't avoid it with someone who's...like that with you. All the time. Anyway. It's not a thing.

SAM: Seriously, what was your trick?

DARA: There was no trick. I was really, really grumpy on a call one time because it came in during a

	match and I missed the penalty, but most people wouldn't consider that endearing. Are you so bored by silly season you're hoping for office drama?
SAM:	You've talked how many times about how obnoxious and annoying and insufferable –
DARA:	Which is all true.
SAM:	I believe you. I'm just… entertained.
DARA:	Have you got popcorn for this afternoon and all the handholding I'm going to have to do?
SAM:	Dara's guide to life. The IT department can't help it, they were born that way, and it's important to remember that before killing them. You're a terrible influence.
DARA:	(*Beat*) So, how was your weekend?
SAM:	I put my work phone in the freezer. Inside a bag, obviously – I didn't even look at a news story until Sunday night.
DARA:	Except for the cats.
SAM:	The cats were everywhere, Dara, the only way I could have avoided them is by wearing a blindfold and being suddenly deaf. But I avoided everything else.
DARA:	That sounds wonderful. Next weekend I'm not looking at a single screen.

Dara opens one of the newspapers

SAM: Is Jo around today?

DARA: Working from home – some awful database cleanse image manipulation thing, we've apparently needed to do for the last year. We have too many stock photos – after this we'll have less. Fewer. I couldn't bear to ask any questions, because after thirty seconds or so of it being explained my brain started attempting to escape via my ears. It has to be done and it's really important and it's a lot of maths.

SAM: So, you're saying *I* should volunteer to do the press lines on taxable benefits and deductions then?

DARA: I think I am, yeah. If you don't mind.

SAM: You had a hard weekend, so just this once.

DARA: You're really all right, you know that? I don't care what they say.

SAM: (*Beat*) What are you looking for in there?

DARA: Wanted to see if we made the print.

SAM: And not online? Just how bad of an interview was it?

DARA: On a scale of one to Tom Cruise jumping on the couch?

SAM: That's not a scale, that's reversed, one is bad –

DARA: You know what I mean. Maybe a six. Definitely not as eye–catching as I promised when I was doing the dance of the seven veils to get the interview. In she walks and immediately says, "First of all, I'm not that interesting, and I don't really have anything to say." The look the journalist gave me – I've never seen someone look so betrayed unless they were married. We're not magicians, how are we supposed to work in these conditions?

SAM: Don't they know who you are?

DARA: I'm hoping we just got bumped to later this week. I mean, they sent a photographer, so you'd think they'd want to use it, but... Maybe they'll call later today, and apologise –

SAM: Apologise. Yes. That sounds like a thing that would happen. I've known dozens of journalists to call and apologise.

DARA: They'll apologise, and it will be the lead story on Wednesday, and they're sending me a bottle of something special as a thank you, and – just let me have this.

SAM: After this weekend, no way you want to be the lead story.

DARA: I was indulging a fantasy. But no, obviously, that would mean a *major* fuck–up, and I don't think she said anything interesting enough for that, thank god. At least, I hope not, we've got enough to deal with.

SAM: But it is August. And they'll all be in the mood to give us a kicking after Cat–Gate.

DARA: Let me make one thing clear – it's not a Gate. It is most definitely not a Gate. A poorly timed FOI release and a charity jumping on the bandwagon because they see a chance for an easy headline and that sweet, sweet name recognition, does not equal a Gate.

SAM: Are you insulted on Nixon's behalf?

DARA: You know what...say what you will, but he *earned* his scandal. He put the time in. We don't have the dedication or commitment to be even moderately evil, not if it means staying later than six.

SAM: What kind of monster wants to work later than six. You have to have *standards*, Dara.

DARA: Very funny.

Pause

SAM: You know, Jo asked if we should retweet the poll.

DARA: Because what, we want to keep the story going for a *third* day? (*Beat*) You said no.

Alex enters, followed by Vick.

SAM: It would show people we have a sense of humour.

DARA: But we don't.

SAM: Speak for yourself.

DARA: We're an institution, people don't want us to have a sense of humour. It would be funny for a second, and then it makes you wonder if you need to start stockpiling toilet paper. We're like your Dad – people want to laugh at the fact that we're not funny, and then have us continue being a stable, reliable, boring presence in their lives. All going well they should never have to think about us at all.

ALEX: Is that an official statement, or –

DARA: Sorry.

ALEX: I mean, it's Vick's first day, I want the place to seem interesting, and then you go and summarise our entire media strategy in one devastating sentence.

DARA: (*Beat*) *This* is Vick?

VICK: The one, the only. Happy to be here.

DARA: But you're –

SAM: The bane of your fucking life? The ruiner of perfectly pleasant Saturday afternoons? The 'just calling' with some tricky bullshit a minute before the office closes?

DARA: No. I mean, yes. Obviously. But –

VICK: Obviously?

ALEX: It's safe to say your reputation precedes you.

SAM: You know that painting The Scream? (*Gestures*) That's how Dara looked every time you called.

ALEX: That was only sometimes true.

VICK: It wasn't quite the effect I was hoping for, but / okay.

SAM: Oh, we know what effect you were –

ALEX: In any case, from now on you can put those life-ruining skills to work for us instead of against us.

SAM: Don't worry, it's not like you had a nickname.

VICK: You gave us nicknames?

DARA: No.

SAM: *I* gave you nicknames. For some reason no one else will use them, because something something professionalism.

ALEX: And on that note – I'm really sorry about this Vick, I was hoping to have more time on your first day, but things got away from me, and I have to go do my very favourite job.

VICK: Do I want to know what that is?

DARA: The reading of the risk register.

SAM: All the things we don't want anyone to find out about because we'll be on the front page every day for a week

ALEX: And we'll also have burned the building down while sexually harassing all of our staff and accidentally facilitating tax evasion. You know, the kind of thing that wakes me up in a cold sweat at four in the morning. (*Beat*) Dara will get you set up with your desk and laptop and so on, and I'll be back this afternoon.

VICK: Great. Thanks.

ALEX: Maybe we should add pest control to the list after this weekend. (*Beat*) Dara?

DARA: What? (*Beat*) No. I'll quit.

ALEX: You say that every time.

DARA: And I always mean it.

ALEX: And yet. Be nice. (*To everyone*) See you later.

Alex leaves

VICK: So, where am I?

DARA: (*Beat*) You can pick a desk – we don't have set ones, so you can move around as needed... If that's a –

VICK: Look, I –

DARA: I've got your laptop and headset and your mobile here, just have to log in and you should be good to go.

VICK: I'm getting the feeling / you didn't know?

DARA: There's a list of databases and inboxes and so on, you'll have to change the passwords, but they should all be set up, I certainly yelled at them enough.

VICK: And?

DARA: And your twitter pic is you with a pineapple in front of your face, so of course I didn't know.

SAM: Know what?

DARA: / Nothing

VICK: Did you think I talked to everyone like that?

DARA: No, I thought you were strange. (*Beat*) What? There are enough oddball journalists out there to fill a moderately–sized shark tank, so you didn't really stand out.

SAM: I wouldn't go that far.

DARA: And it was ages ago.

SAM: What was ages ago?

Pause

VICK: Nothing.

DARA: See?

SAM: Oh yeah, because this definitely resembles nothing. I see nothings just like this all the time.

Phone rings.

SAM: Hello, press office, Sam speaking. (*Pause*) I don't think that's something we can – (*Beat*) No, I'll look into it for you, but...probably best not to get your hopes up. (*Beat*) I'll be in touch. (*Hangs up*). Drivetime – they want to "give us an opportunity to tell our side of the pest control story."

DARA: That'll be a no – I want it to go away, not –

SAM: I know, I did say. But we try to place stuff with them all the time, I don't want to piss them off.

DARA: Fine. Wait half an hour and then say no, make them think we considered it.

VICK: So, pest control is a thing?

SAM: A freedom of information request went out on Friday, saying our pest control costs had tripled. Which would have been a nothing little Saturday story, except –

DARA: Except that the local cats and dogs home tweeted that they would *give* us a cat, for free, to help cut costs, and then they ran a public poll, to help choose the cat, and of course everyone picked that up and ran with it. They had vox pops running on news 24, we went viral for twenty-eight hours, we were the front page of two Sunday papers and I hate August.

SAM: Dara was the on-call media officer, hence the cheery Monday morning mood.

DARA: Anyway. Moving on.

VICK: Right.

DARA: Those passwords won't reset themselves.

SCENE TWO

The press office. Mid–afternoon, the same day.

VICK: I've logged in.

SAM: Congratulations.

VICK: I can hear the sarcasm, but I'm taking it.

SAM: I've seen better people than you defeated by the system. (*Beat*) I meant the IT system, that wasn't a political statement.

VICK: You can express an opinion, I won't run to my editor. I'm on your side now.

SAM: For now. And who knows, you survived the IT, the food didn't get you, maybe you will stay.

VICK: Maybe?

SAM: The last journalist who tried made it two weeks.

VICK: Really?

SAM: It's not for the faint–hearted. And no one hated *them*.

VICK: Dara doesn't hate me.

SAM: Is that so?

VICK: I promise you, I haven't done anything to make myself hated.

SAM: But you did something?

VICK: Well done, you caught me, now I'm going to tell you all about our torrid affair.

SAM: Torrid? Really?

VICK: Have you *ever* heard anyone use that word and mean it?

Dara enters

SAM: So, it was just an affair then?

DARA: It wasn't anything like that!

Pause

VICK: Look, we weren't –

DARA: What exactly have you been saying?

VICK: I wasn't – I was just about to explain –

DARA: Kissing a few times at a wedding does not constitute – unless you don't know what an affair is? Which, one, I'm pretty sure it's more involved than that, and two a press officer needs to know what words actually mean.

VICK: No, I know, I wasn't –

DARA: Also affairs don't involve one party acting like some weird wanted criminal and never sharing their full name. (*Beat*) I mean, I've heard.

SAM: Ah.

VICK: I didn't *never* share my full name, I just never shared my full name when you were in the vicinity.

DARA: Because what, you were on the Interpol list? Were there drones tracking your every move?

SAM: So *that*'s why you didn't know that you'd... with –

DARA: You didn't work that out like eight sentences ago? I thought you lived for the drama.

VICK: It was all a bit rushed – Dara, Vick, Vick, Dara, and then almost immediately straight on to the – (*off Dara's look*) It didn't come up.

DARA: But you knew *my* name, didn't you? That's why whenever you called me you used to be so... all the time. Wasn't it?

VICK: Yeah, obviously. I did like you, so when I realised... that made you my favourite one to call, what's the –

DARA: Doesn't explain why you were in such a rush to tell my – *our* colleagues all about –

VICK: I was about to say that there was nothing *to* say when you came in.

DARA: It didn't sound like you were saying there was nothing, it sounded like –

An explosion

Close enough that the walls shake and the lights flicker, but not so close anything is damaged. The sound is as loud and frightening as a thunderclap when you're directly underneath it.

There is a long pause.

SAM: Was that in the building?

DARA: I don't know. I don't think so.

VICK: You don't think so?

DARA: That felt strong enough to flatten a – but we're still here, so –

A phone starts to ring. Followed by a second, and a third. For the rest of the scene, unless otherwise stated, the phones ring continuously, ringing almost the instant the characters hang up.

VICK: "I don't think so" isn't going to work –

DARA: As a press line, I know.

Dara's mobile rings.

SAM: What do we say?

DARA: Just...just – take details, take details and call them back.

VICK: Not say *anything*?

DARA: We can't, we don't know anything. (*Picks up*) Hello, press / Dara speaking

SAM: Hello, press office / Sam speaking

DARA: I'll have to / call you back

SAM: If I can / take your details

DARA: Yes, I know that / but I'm afraid all I can do right now is take your number and call you back once...once I have something to issue. In an email will be fine.

Dara's phone rings again

SAM: (*Writing it down*) 083 331 62491. Goodbye. (*Picks up next call*). Hello, press office, Sam speaking. (*Beat*) I'll have to get back to you on that. (*Beat*) As soon as possible, yes.

DARA: Vick. What are you doing?

VICK: I... I've never taken a press call before.

DARA: So? You must have *made* thousands of them over the years, it's not like it's hard.

SAM: I know you'll want to publish immediately. I understand that. / We're looking into your query and will be back in touch as soon, as soon as we can. And that's all I can say right now.

DARA: Go look out a window at least, so we have some idea what we're dealing with. (*Picks up phone. Vick leaves.*) Hello, press, Dara speaking. Nick, hello, yes. (*Beat*) Yes, we're looking into that, and we expect to issue a line shortly. / Yes, I have your email. Yes, as soon as.

SAM: Hello, press office, Sam speaking. (*Beat*) Yes, we are aware of an (*searches for the right word*) event. We're hoping – I mean, we're planning – we'll be issuing something soon. No, I can't say how soon. (*Beat*) Well obviously not *days*. I'm afraid I can't stay on the phone, we're very busy, but I'll be in touch once we issue. charlie dot gray at the hyphen times dot co dot uk, yes. (*Hangs up*).

DARA: An event?

SAM: What would you call it?

DARA: Not an 'event' – Beyoncé releasing a new album is an event – maybe an incident?

SAM: That's what the police always say.

DARA: So?

SAM: We don't want to scare people.

DARA: Did you hear...that ship has well and truly sailed, people *are* scared, and I don't think our describing a massive fuck–off kaboom like it's a special shopping discount is going to reassure *anyone*.

SAM: You're criticising me for calling it an event when you just used the word 'kaboom?'

DARA: Just – answer the phone.

Vick returns mid–stream.

SAM: Hello, press office, Sam speaking. / Yes, we have been getting a lot of calls. (*Beat*) Not at this point, no, but we expect to issue in the near future. As soon as we have something to share, you'll be on the list, I promise. ...I think that's a safe assumption, yes, but I can't say for –

DARA: Alex, thank god. Yes, I'm fine, we're all – we're all okay, no one was hurt. Where are you? (*Pause*) No, don't come back, we don't know... It might not be safe. (*Beat*) They're saying what on twitter? You're breaking up. (*Beat*) You're serious? No, we haven't heard anything about any –

Both phone calls end abruptly. All the phones stop ringing.

SAM: What just –

VICK: They'll have brought down the network.

DARA: They?

VICK: Police, security, whatever

SAM: Why would they do that – it's a fucking emergency.

Pause

DARA: Because of mobile phone triggers. They'll be worried about someone using a mobile phone trigger.

VICK: Yeah. That'll be it.

Long pause

DARA: Alex was saying – I *think* Alex was saying there's speculation that it's a terrorist attack, that's what they were saying on twitter. (*Beat*) I shouldn't have sent you outside, are you okay?

VICK: There's smoke everywhere. (*Beat*) I'm fine, I didn't even open the door, just looked out the window. Something... Dara, something really serious happened out there.

SAM: Yeah. (*Beat*) We're on TV.

Pause as they look at the TV screen.

SAM: Jesus Christ, that's half the main building.

VICK: It hasn't collapsed though, it's still –

SAM: You can barely tell behind the smoke and –

DARA: It looks like they're evacuating people.

Pause

DARA: Okay, the networks are down, but I want you both to write a message to your families telling them you're all right, so it's ready to go the second they come back up. You won't get the chance otherwise, it's going to be a long afternoon.

All three start typing on their phones.

DARA: For now at least, I think we should stay where we are. Everything's working, there's no smoke, there's power, it seems safe, so... Sam, collect all the loose phone and laptop chargers in a grab bag, so we can go mobile if we have to. In the meantime, make sure to plug your laptops in, so

	you've got a full charge, and if either of you have one of those battery packs for your phone, plug it in right now.
SAM:	Do you think we'll have to leave?
DARA:	I don't know – we still don't know what we're dealing with, and it seems like it's just in the main building but it makes sense to prepare. Alex didn't think there was any immediate threat, but we got cut off before – so who knows.
SAM:	You think there's been – you think people have –
VICK:	Look at it.
DARA:	It could just be a hell of a lot of smoke and nothing more, but –
VICK:	Just smoke?
DARA:	Okay, it's almost certainly *not* just smoke, but we shouldn't assume – people hyperventilate on social media all the time, it doesn't necessarily mean that –
VICK:	We have to say *something*.
DARA:	I know that. (*Searches through phone*) I've got the number for the police press office in here somewhere, I'll call them, find out what they're saying. We need to be aligned – we can't contradict them.
VICK:	And in the meantime?

DARA: We're aware of an ongoing incident and we're working to contain the situation.

VICK: Do we know it's ongoing? If we say it is, and it isn't – everyone freaks and then –

DARA: Okay, we're aware of an incident and we're working with emergency services to con –

SAM: To manage it. Contain sounds too...

DARA: Danger is imminent, run the fuck away, you're right, you only have to contain something if it's trying to escape and we don't want people to –

VICK: To what, be frightened? I think that's something we can just assume at this point.

DARA: To panic. We've got three different buildings with staff in them here, if they all get scared and start running around and – we have to sound like we know what we're doing.

VICK: We also have to sound like we're acknowledging the reality of the giant fuck off ball of flame. Otherwise they'll think the press office is having a collective dissociative episode.

DARA: We are working with emergency services to manage the situation. Sam, you've got it?

SAM: Yeah.

DARA: Prep a twitter card, we want it to look as official as possible, complete with our logo. And Alex needs to know what we're saying, so get it in an email, and it's the first thing you send when the network –

The phones start ringing.

DARA: (*Starts to call the police*) As soon as it's ready, we'll issue that way and just refer everyone to the twitter account. Get Jo to do it, we've got too many calls, send an email with the text and –

VICK: Hello, press. / Yes, we are aware of an incident, we're working to contain –

SAM: I'm on it. Do you want me to start monitoring?

VICK: To manage the situation.

DARA: Yeah, if you can. Anything too outlandish, let me know.

VICK: I'm sorry, that's all I can tell you.

SAM: What does outlandish even look like right now?

DARA: Well, I don't know, if they say a green fairy is dancing on the roof, maybe ask a few follow-up questions.

VICK: I can assure you, we haven't said any such thing. We're not in a position to – we're not issuing detailed statements at this time, so – he hung up.

SAM: / Press office, Sam speaking.

DARA: What was he saying?

VICK: Something about a machine gun.

SAM: / I can't answer speculative questions like that.

DARA: What?

VICK: That two men with machine guns had entered the —

DARA: That's not — Alex would have said something.

VICK: / Assuming Alex knew.

SAM: I understand it's a developing story, but I can't give you answers to...to hypothetical — well fuck you too.

VICK: Hung up?

SAM: Yeah. (*Looks at screen*). Jo started working on the card before we even, so... It'll be up in a minute or two. And Alex is happy with the line.

DARA: Vick?

VICK: Yeah.

DARA: Lock the door. Just in case.

Pause

VICK: Lock the — yeah. (*Goes to do so*).

SAM: You think maybe it's —

DARA: It's probably nothing, Alex would have said, Alex would have told us to run if there was any... but can't be too careful.

VICK: Press office, Vick speaking.

SAM: Should we even be here? Shouldn't we be leaving, if –

DARA: And go where? It's all smoke out there, you've seen it, and we don't know what we're dealing with, so –

VICK: I'm sorry, what?

DARA: Hi. Yes, yes, this is Dara. Yes, I'm calling from the press office, it's about the…the incident we're dealing with here, I wanted to check what your line is, to make sure we're saying the same thing, we're on the same – yes, I'll hold.

VICK: You're asking me about a *cat*?

Pause. Sam listens in, ignoring the phones. Dara turns away, continuing the call to the police.

VICK: No, I can't issue a line about a cat today… I understand you think a ginger cat is an important story, but we're dealing with a – just email your request in. (*Beat*) I don't know – when we get to it. No, I don't know when that will be. (*Beat*) Your deadline is just going to have to wait, we're too busy today for cats, this a no cat press office.

SAM: The line is out on twitter. On the incident, not the cats.

VICK: Right.

SAM: So just refer people to that, and don't take any other questions, don't get drawn into some – press office, Sam speaking. / Alex hi, no I'm fine, we're fine, Dara's on the line with the police right now.

VICK: Press, Vick speaking. You've seen our statement on twitter, yes? Well that's as far as. (*Beat*) An "unofficial" source? Well I can't – we can't – I'll get back to you.

Dara and Vick hang up their calls.

SAM: Yeah, we put the line up online and – no we haven't sent anything to staff yet, I thought that was – nothing sent over email, no, they must have forgot. / Yeah, I've got a pen.

DARA: Police say it's not a terrorist incident, though they haven't said how they know. Anyway, I think I know where our machine gun fantasies are coming from. See? (*Shows Vick on the phone*). This idiot is streaming the whole experience and sharing every random suggestion he thinks of.

SAM: I've got it. Yeah, I'll work it out – we'll send in the next few minutes, I'll get Dara to look it over before I hit send. (*Hangs up*)

VICK: Who is he?

DARA: He's... someone in payroll, I – Sam could you have a look? I can't remember the name, and I'm going to need it when I go over there to beat him to death with his mobile phone. "People are saying" there are men with machine guns, and "people are saying" the roof has fallen in and decapitated a third of the staff and "people are saying" every moronic thing that comes into their heads, because what this situation needs is a few thousand even more terrified people, since they always make *great* decisions.

SAM: (*To Dara*) Can you read this – it's for internal?

VICK: Hello, press, / Vick speaking.

DARA: Why are *we* – never mind. Same as the press line but with a "stay put unless otherwise instructed if you are in a location unaffected by the incident whatever the fuck it is?"

SAM: ...Basically

DARA: You know it'll show up online the second we –

SAM: Yeah, but we don't have a choice, we have to tell –

DARA: / Yeah. Just get it out.

VICK: You've seen our statement? I can't say any further at this time. (*New call*) Press, Vick speaking. We've issued a statement online, I'll refer you to that in the first instance. Any updates will be posted there. (*New call*) Press, Vick speaking... I'm afraid I can't answer specifics right now, you'll just have to – that's all I can tell you. (*New call*) Press office, Vick speaking / no, I think it's safe to say future operations will be affected, I can't say more than – I would refer you to our statement online. Well

	just search for our name and you'll find us on twitter.
SAM:	Got it. Enda.
DARA:	Enda who?
SAM:	McGrath, he's on one of those panels for something we all have to champion, I can't remember.
DARA:	You got a number?
SAM:	Yeah. (*Hands it over*)
VICK:	Press, Vick speaking. No, you're right, I absolutely can't answer that question. Yes, it will just have to wait. Yes, I am being unhelpful, but if it's any consolation, I promise you no one else is getting any answers either.
DARA:	Take a look at the inbox, would you, it's probably carnage in there right now. This fucker's not picking up, I guess his audience is too – Enda, hi, it's Dara from the press office. I'm afraid you're causing us a little bit of a problem right now, and I'm going to need you to – I understand that you're trying to help, but it's not *actually* helping, it's causing us more problems because – no, I *don't* think this is a chance for us to demonstrate our commitment to transparency, if you could just –

Vick watches Dara listen to a diatribe

VICK:	Let me?

DARA: Why?

VICK: Just – (*takes the phone*) Enda, mate, look, I understand what you're trying to do. We've all got families, and they want to know we're all right. But every time you share one of your "guesses" about what might have happened, we get a dozen over-excited journalists on the line, all *pining* for some bloodshed because that will make it a *real* story, and they don't believe us when we say it's bullshit – which it is by the way, and the police are saying so – because you're out here being a citizen journalist. And it's my first day, so, you know, things are already a lot more stressful than I was expecting, and this job was supposed to mean a nice quiet life. (*Beat*) Thanks. (*Hangs up*)

SAM: Good news.

DARA: Actually good news?

SAM: Most of the inbox can be dealt with by emailing them the statement, Jo can do that while we cover the phones, plus two queries about the cat, which we'll ignore for now. Also, Alex emailed to say we've got confirmation we can stay in place, it's safe here.

DARA: Thanks. And thanks. Guess we better strap in. Anyone got any snacks?

VICK: I can split a banana?

DARA: Press, Dara speaking. Hi Caimin. (*Sam reacts to*

hearing the name, starts listening in) Yes, that is our statement at this time. We'll update as and when we can. (*Beat*) I can't speak to anything about maintenance issues or – it's far too early to – if you print that it will be nothing but unfounded speculation and your editor will be hearing from us. (*Beat*) Of course we'll be looking into the causes of the incident, but at a future date, now is not the time – no, I can't put you on the phone with the fire team, they're busy, but if you print a word of this before you have any reliable information, I will immediately call your editor and – no, the fact that someone said it in a dark corner of the internet somewhere does not make it reliable, it doesn't make it anything. (*Beat*) I am too busy to argue with you, but if you hit publish, you will hear from us immediately.

VICK: Bad?

DARA: Nineteen dead because of faults in our gas and electrical system – Caimin claims, anyway – and of course we don't even know if anyone's been hurt, let alone... It could just be someone didn't close a door or they did and they shouldn't have and now if anyone's dead they're going to have negligent homicide all over the fucking press before we even know what happened, before the families have been told that their – that's how they'll find out that... If that's the story it won't matter *what* we say. (*To Sam*) Keep Caimin Finlay's account up for monitoring – Jo can do it – and if there's even a word of –

SAM: Yeah.

VICK: Press, Vick speaking. / Yes, that is our current statement.

DARA: I've got to call Alex.

SAM: Yeah. (*Beat*) Press office, Sam speaking.

Lights dim as the phone calls continue.

SCENE THREE

Lights up.

Hours later. Traffic on the phone lines has slowed. Everyone is worn out.

SAM: Do you have any food?

VICK: We ate the one banana three hours ago.

SAM: So you don't have, like, mints or something?

VICK: Sorry.

DARA: I might have a snack in my locker somewhere. Dried fruit, I think.

SAM: Thanks, but –

DARA: Dried fruit not do it for you?

SAM: I want something really filling that I don't have to digest in any way.

VICK: It's like the morning after a wedding.

DARA: What kind of weddings have you been at?

Phone rings. They all wait to see who is willing to pick up.

VICK: Hello, press. (*Beat*) No, we won't… let me check – access for a press photographer?

DARA: They're all standing at the gate anyway, what –

VICK: To the actual –

DARA: No. Even if they'd let one in, which, they won't,

we'd get sworn at for suggesting it. And one of us would have to escort them, make sure they don't get crushed by a falling ladder or rubble or whatever, and we're not – tomorrow is going to be… insane, no one is staying three hours late for that

VICK: Sorry, that's a no. (*Beat*) I *can* answer straightaway, because even if I asked, *and* they said yes, we couldn't do it, we don't have the capacity to bring you in, so – rude.

DARA: They're busy, they're on deadline, they do that – I've been hung up on eleven times today. Or it might have been eighty–seven, I'm not sure.

Long Pause.

SAM: I can't believe we've been sitting down this whole time.

DARA: Maybe we should book in a massage therapist to come in tomorrow – or have someone scatter some essential oils. They won't do anything, but the place would smell nice.

SAM: See, I say attack the problem at source – let's just shoot up. Won't have any problems staying awake then.

DARA: An official spokesperson said.

VICK: Please, it's not like any of them talk to us long enough to notice anyway. Do you think it'll be bad, tomorrow?

DARA: Chances are...I don't know. I'd start praying for something really eye–catching and non–lethal.

SAM: You always say this.

DARA: I'm telling you if a brand new volcanic island just appeared off the coast of Scotland, that would distract everyone, and we wouldn't need to feel guilty, because no one would be dead.

VICK: I'm not sure it's quite the front page news story you –

DARA: You're missing the point. I'm not comfortable wishing for bad things to happen to people. I'd much prefer if we got bumped for a *good* reason – an everyone is looking at an optical illusion dress reason, not that a prominent public figure died in a plane crash.

VICK: Good news never drives out the bad – you never heard "if it bleeds it leads?" We have brains that are really, really good at remembering where the angry toothy things live, as opposed to the pretty butterflies, because if we weren't good at it, well –

DARA: That doesn't *have* to be true.

VICK: Only half as many babies die before their first birthday as thirty years ago, globally. Have you ever seen that on the front page? I mean, look, when they find the cure for cancer, I'll happily be proven wrong, but in the meantime, this is not a strategy.

DARA: I know that. I need to talk to Alex. We still don't really know what we're dealing with, other than, you know, the terrible. (*Beat*) One of you can go, if you want – go home, go to the pub, get some sleep or a drink or whatever. It's quietened down enough.

VICK: (*Beat*) I don't have far to go, so, if you want to –

SAM: Thanks, I'll – but (*to Dara*) you're the one with the long trip, so –

DARA: I have to talk to Alex first though – maybe bring in some doughnuts tomorrow.

SAM: Sure

Sam prepares to leave – gathering coat, bag and so on.

VICK: How far do you have to go?

DARA: Best part of an hour. It's fine, just, you know, long. Long and with only intermittent mobile phone signal, which might actually be a relief. That ring tone is starting to hurt my ears.

VICK: You could – if it's going to be late, you could –

Alex enters

ALEX: You all look like a bomb went off. (*Pause*) Sorry, not funny. Long day.

VICK: Yeah.

ALEX: Vick, well done. You're still here, not run away screaming yet.

VICK:	It definitely crossed my mind.
DARA:	But with all the emergency services outside, it's not like you'd have gotten far.
VICK:	Maybe tomorrow.
ALEX:	(*Pause*) Well done. All of you.
SAM:	We just sat here.
ALEX:	Even over the phones, I've heard enough to know just sitting here wasn't easy.
VICK:	Do we know – do we know how many died?
ALEX:	Eight. The families are being told at the moment – once that's done the emergency services will announce the names. Probably first thing in the morning. At the hospital.
DARA:	Who – can you tell us who –

The phone rings. When Dara picks up, for the first time we hear the journalist's voice, which is warm and friendly.

DARA:	Press, Dara speaking.
NICK:	Dara, hi, it's Nick here from the BBC.
DARA:	Hi Nick, what can I do for you?
NICK:	You must all have been rushed off your feet with today – is everyone all right over there?
DARA:	We've definitely had easier days, but... we're managing.

NICK: I know you must be dying to go home and sleep it off, but... I just wanted to ask, we've been hearing stories about a school group that were in for a visit, and –

DARA: (*Trying not to show a reaction*) A school group?

NICK: Yes, they were in for a tour, and we wanted to see if they –

DARA: Just a second.

ALEX: No.

DARA: No?

ALEX: It's not any of them – their coach service picked them up. Couple of hours late, but they're on their way home.

DARA: (*So relieved it shows*). Right. (*Beat*) Nick, they're making their way home as we speak. I don't know how long a drive it is, but they'll... They'll just be a little late.

NICK: Maybe they'll even miss rush hour.

DARA: Yeah.

NICK: And I wanted to say, your whole team has...you were all very helpful today and it can't have been easy. So, thank you.

DARA: (*Breaking*) You're welcome. (*Hangs up. Pause*) Sorry, sorry everyone, just... Just too much for a second there.

ALEX: Only a few minutes more, and then you can go home.

DARA: Yeah.

ALEX: I'll draft a message to all staff tonight – it'll go out in the morning. In the teams where people have... the managers will do a ring round tonight, make sure everyone who worked closely with them is told before the names come out in the press.

DARA: Do you...do you want me to help with the wording –

ALEX: If you can do a review, read it over for me, before, say, midnight... That'd help. The Boss will look at it overnight.

DARA: I can do that.

ALEX: I'll cover the out of hours tonight, and the rest of you – go home.

SAM: What about the interviews?

ALEX: Interviews?

VICK: A couple of people did interviews – nothing much, just... once they were told they were free to go they had to walk out past by three different cameras, so – they got grabbed on the way.

ALEX: That's a generous assumption. It's just as likely they enjoyed the attention. You'd be surprised.

People don't think, especially when they're fired up.

VICK: It's never hard to get an interview immediately after a disaster, I know that much.

ALEX: Well, we're not going to do anything about it, no one's thinking clearly tonight, not when they've been locked in for hours, all keyed up by the crisis. We'll wait until things have calmed down and maybe send out a gentle reminder about referring questions to the press office. In the meantime, all of you, you've done more than enough, go home. (*Beat*) Actually, Dara, can you – I've been locked up in the Chief Exec's office since midday, can you wait five minutes while I go to the –

DARA: Yeah, of course.

ALEX: Thanks.

Alex leaves. Followed by Sam.

SAM: (*Before exiting*) I'll see you tomorrow.

VICK: (*To Dara*) You all right?

Pause

DARA: Not really. When all the phones were ringing, they drowned out everything I was – eight people are dead. And we have to come back tomorrow and answer questions so the press can *use* them to sell papers and go viral and we'll have to find a slant on it that doesn't make us look completely terrible, even though it won't matter, even though they're already saying we...you've seen it, how it's all our fault and, and, and I have to sit on a train now and there'll be people talking about it and reading about it and eight people we *know* –

VICK: Want to get a drink?

DARA: What?

VICK: There's nothing I can do about – I *can* buy you a drink.

DARA: Can you? Yes.

VICK: Is that a yes I can, or yes I will –

DARA: It's a yes! Don't get all copy editor red pen on me, just –

VICK: Yes.

DARA: And I want another banana.

VICK: I'll see what I can do.

DARA: (*Pause*) Thanks.

Alex returns.

ALEX: Go. I want you out of here. (*Beat*) I'll have a draft in about an hour, so, if you can try to review it by –

DARA: Let's say eleven. I'll call you and we can talk it through.

ALEX: Good. Now go.

The phone rings as Dara and Vick leave.

ALEX: Press office, Alex speaking, how can I help? (*Beat*) You know perfectly well that we can't issue that kind of information, not at this point in time, so you'll just have to wait until we – well goodnight then.

LIGHTS DOWN

SCENE FOUR

The next morning. The office.

Dara works on a laptop.

Vick enters.

VICK: You're here.

DARA: Yeah.

VICK: I thought you'd be – I was expecting to see –

DARA: I didn't really sleep. And you know, lots to do.

VICK: Yeah. You didn't want / to –

DARA: Didn't want to wake you, no. I figured one of us should get to – I just had to go.

VICK: Right.

DARA: Look, I appreciate everything you – I do – but I needed to clear my head.

VICK: Okay. (*Beat*) You're not worried people will notice?

DARA: Notice?

VICK: Well you're wearing the same –

DARA: Oh. No. Desk drawer, I have clothes in my desk drawer for emergencies. By which I always meant soup spill emergencies, not... anyway. I was going to get changed as soon as I – but then

	I was checking all the coverage and Alex asked me to… I got distracted.
VICK:	I should have thought of that.
DARA:	It's always good to have – you don't know when there'll be a crisis and you'll be dragged in to advise and need to resemble a competent professional.
VICK:	Right.
DARA:	I'm saying you should bring in clothes tomorrow and –
VICK:	Right.
DARA:	And, no one's going to notice anything after yesterday, and even if they do –
VICK:	You'll?
DARA:	If they ask, there's nothing to be… I'll do something radical and tell them the truth. I slept on the sofa, or, well, didn't sleep, so it's not as though – I live a million miles away from here, everyone will just assume that you were being decent.
VICK:	Right.
DARA:	And… it's no one's business even if we had given in and decided to – not that we did, but *if* we did it wouldn't matter what they think.
VICK:	Sorry, given in? Did you *want* to –

DARA: I didn't say that.

VICK: I know you didn't say that, but you...seem on edge.

DARA: No, no, I'm not – this is actually my usual degree of edge.

VICK: Really? I'm not making you nervous right now?

DARA: Yes, really, there's no need for a tone, I'm not... I didn't go home with you last night because I expected anything to –

VICK: I get that. But your office did explode literally yesterday and kill people, so it seems like you would have *more* than your usual edge, and I'm going to stop saying that word now.

DARA: I meant –

VICK: I know what you meant, but it's natural to be... off. You knew some of them.

DARA: Not well. Just –

VICK: But enough.

DARA: I cried.

VICK: I didn't mean to –

DARA: Last night, after you, after we... when we agreed I'd sleep on the sofa... I ended up lying there, hoping your flatmate wouldn't come in, because I was a massive fake, eyes streaming like taps when I wasn't sad, I had no reason, I just –

VICK: You had reason.

DARA: No, but you see, I didn't, because I wasn't thinking about those people, I wasn't thinking about eight fucking body bags being carried out of the building in a line, I was thinking about myself. And I know I shouldn't have been, I know I should have been thinking about... it's like, I can't feel it yet, I'm too – (*makes an effort*) – did you read the overnight stuff?

VICK: Some of it. After three or four, it's kind of pointless.

DARA: Alex wants a summary to show the Boss in half an hour and it's fucking awful. (*Beat*) We're the front page. I've never had a front page for anything, and now there's been two in a row, and today's is all about how we not–so–accidentally killed people. Front pages are for riots and wars and sexy murders, not – we're not *supposed* to be the front page.

VICK: It led the morning bulletin as well.

DARA: Of course it did.

VICK: A story like this in August, it's a gift for them, and for us... really bad timing.

DARA: Yeah, our massive fuck–off explosion was really inconsiderate that way. You know, I spend half my life trying to explain the importance of timing when it comes to big media announcements, that you can't just fling a press release out and expect

	results, and they always nodded and didn't really believe me...you think any of this will change their minds?
VICK:	I wouldn't bet on it. Are you sure you should be working today?
DARA:	And abandon the rest of you to the vultures? No. This is what I always do. I deal with the crisis, whatever it is –
VICK:	Cats.
DARA:	Cats, yes, exactly. We got two more emails about them overnight you know. Anyway, I dealt with that story, I resolved it, I issued the line on every channel you can think of, batted back all the interview requests, and then... I downloaded. Poor Sam got an earful yesterday morning.
VICK:	But probably used to it by now.
DARA:	Yeah, despite how it may seem, this is not normal. I spend most of my time begging for a half inch of column space, not trying to correct every front page in the country.
VICK:	Yeah, I saw the email. Does the Boss really want us to demand four separate corrections?
DARA:	Yeah. It's one of the things Alex is going to talk to him about.
VICK:	You'd think he'd be more worried about all the resignation talk. And you know they won't do it.

DARA: Oh, of course I know. But if they're set on it my opinion doesn't matter.

VICK: So, even though we're going to have more than enough to do with all the follow up – we can't say that actually, we'd prefer to avoid picking a fight, and focus on what we can control, like prepping for interviews.

DARA: Are you mad?

VICK: You know I'm right, seeking corrections is a road to nowhere.

DARA: I meant interviews.

VICK: We need to reassure people, show them we have things under control.

DARA: Do we? (*Beat*) I mean, we do, but –

VICK: But not so much you want to put someone out there?

DARA: They're already demanding the Boss' head on a platter – all that has to happen is he makes a weird face or doesn't know how to answer a question for four whole seconds, and then we're screwed. That fifteen seconds on twitter will be all anyone watches.

VICK: As opposed to yesterday's delightful clip of half the windows on the ground floor blowing out?

DARA: (*Pause*) I forgot about that one. Or maybe I just blanked it – it's not even eight o'clock, and the phones have already been ringing.

VICK: Why don't we tell them all to fuck off and just skip the country?

DARA: Not so much fun on the other side, is it? We could run off to an island somewhere.

VICK: A brand new volcanic island?

DARA: Did I talk about that?

VICK: Your dream good news story that means everyone leaves us alone, yeah, little bit.

DARA: I can't keep track of anything we talked about, we might as well be perfect strangers.

VICK: Which would make running away to an island just a little awkward.

DARA: I'm up for it if you are.

VICK: Really?

Neither of them can look away.

DARA: Obviously, I'm joking.

VICK: Obviously.

DARA: But I'm also not. Last night, it wasn't that I didn't –

VICK: Right.

DARA: Alex and the others will be in soon, and we need to finish reviewing the morning coverage, and come up with a rebuttal for Caimin Finlay's "so it was all their fault story" and –

VICK: Yeah, we do, I know.

DARA: But first –

Dara kisses Vick.

It was intended to be brief – but it doesn't stay that way.

VICK: We could –

DARA: I have to change. Before they –

VICK: Yeah. Yeah, of course.

DARA: So, I'll go do that. (*Beat*) I've just been looking online, so maybe you can check the print? They should have delivered them by now.

VICK: Yeah.

Vick exits

DARA: Well done. Well done. That was a completely necessary and sensible thing to do, that will create a really stable working environment, definitely what I should have – (*the phone rings*). Press office, Dara speaking.

SCENE FIVE

Ten days later. The office is empty.

Dara enters, carrying a flipchart – once the chart has been set up, Dara starts arranging the room for a session.

Vick enters

VICK: Can I help?

DARA: No, it's – I suppose you could arrange the chairs.

VICK: I can do that. (*Beat*) You're avoiding me.

DARA: Sure I am.

VICK: You know what I mean.

DARA: Are we going to argue about the meaning of words again?

VICK: That depends.

DARA: We share an office and for all my working hours I'm never more than six feet away from you. If that's avoiding, I'm really bad at it.

VICK: And yet. (*Beat*) You can relax – I'm not going to – you're safe from me.

DARA: I know that, don't be – we talk every day.

VICK: Yes, your induction programme is very thorough, but I'm not – it's not about that. Which you know. It's the other thing.

DARA: I genuinely don't know how many phone calls and emails and interview requests we've had, and we were trending for three whole days, and Caimin Finlay was chasing me the entire time. That whole week all I ate was bananas and doughnuts, because there wasn't time to have an actual meal, even if I'd wanted one, which I didn't, and it didn't seem to me that when the entire country was united in telling us we should be ashamed of the day we were born and everything we've done on every day since was the time for me to talk about how much I wanted to lick your face.

VICK: You – are you a cat?

DARA: I don't literally want to – I was being – chairs. Please just do them.

VICK: We can move chairs and talk at the same time, that's really a thing we can –

DARA: And yet I'm seeing an awful lot of not moving.

VICK: Fine. (*Moves a chair into position*) Now, can we –

DARA: No.

VICK: No?

DARA: Like I said, it's not – it's not – it's just not helpful. To anything. You *or* me, so.

VICK: Well I disagree.

DARA: So?

VICK: So?

DARA: In case you haven't noticed, you disagree with me like it's your favourite hobby, so yet another time doesn't exactly mean anything.

VICK: Oh that's a blatant exaggeration, we don't disagree about *everything*.

DARA: You're doing it right now!

VICK: (*Enjoying it*) All this time, I thought you were ignoring me because...but it was that you *wanted* me to –

DARA: So?

Alex enters

VICK: So, *that* is brand new information. I could have already done something about that.

DARA: Like what?

ALEX: (*Knowingly interrupting*) Everyone ready for lessons learned?

Pause

DARA: Of course. Jo's covering the phones, so we won't be interrupted. Sam's just getting the print outs, and then we can start.

VICK: Print outs?

DARA: I did a summary of the coverage.

ALEX: All of it?

DARA: Well, not, that would have been...that would take a long, *long* time to print, it's just headlines. The ones I could find anyway.

ALEX: Makes you kind of proud, doesn't it? (*Beat*) We hit so many front pages we don't have room for them all.

DARA: I suppose now it can be our go–to example whenever we have to have one of those "no, you only *think* you want to be on the front page, actually what you really want is a nice three inch column on page four" conversations.

VICK: Let's not flatter ourselves – it *was* August. An unusually large frog will make a headline in August if they get desperate enough. It's not like there's anything else to talk about when everyone is on holiday, the lead story the day before was a pair of cats.

ALEX: It's unkind to bring up Cat–Gate, you know that, Dara's still recovering.

Sam enters

DARA: How many times – it was not a Gate. A Gate is a much more serious bad news story – it doesn't just –

SAM: You realise we only call it that to annoy you, right?

DARA: Yeah and it works, so you can stop any time.

ALEX: Your feline trauma aside, I wanted to do a lessons learned session, so we could talk about... You know, what went well, what didn't, and then propose any changes to the Boss. He wants the bases covered before the inquests start.

VICK: Changes like what?

ALEX: Big, small, it doesn't matter. Anything that might have made it go better – since we clearly weren't prepared.

VICK: Not killing eight people would have been a start.

ALEX: It's something we aim for, as an organisation, but obviously it can't always be avoided. (*Angry*) Try to remember that some of us *knew* them. (*Beat*) It's not going to be the easiest conversation, but Dara's summary gives us somewhere to start. Sam, can you write up the actions?

SAM: It's all about the actions. (*Sam shares the handouts – they each review them for a moment*).

ALEX: It looks even worse when it's all gathered together, doesn't it?

DARA: It was already pretty bad, but, yeah, you could say that.

SAM: Where did they get all their pictures? For that middle page spread of mourning.

VICK: Probably Facebook. They would have gone looking almost as soon as the names were

	announced and pulled off every detail they could find – it's not like anyone would have thought to lock them down.
SAM:	That's... intrusive.
DARA:	They door–stepped the families the day after – I don't think they had scruples about invading people's grief
ALEX:	Could we have done more to...keep that from happening, or warn them that it was a possibility? I don't think anyone wants to see a journalist's face first thing the morning after they've lost –
DARA:	Yeah, but they were already saying we didn't care about anyone who died and it was all our fault and we were to blame – it / would have just seemed...
VICK:	Of course they did.
DARA:	Of course?
VICK:	They weren't going to put "something terrible happened, reasons unclear" on their front page. They needed something they could tell people, a story with a beginning, middle and maybe an end.
DARA:	So, what, they just made it up and hoped for the best?

VICK: No, but... it's probably true. True enough for a headline. If it wasn't would the Boss be 'considering' resignation?

Sam stands by the flipchart, pen in hand.

SAM: Want me to write that up as our official assessment?

ALEX: It hasn't been decided yet.

VICK: No, I didn't mean – I'm saying people fuck up all the time. Take any given moment and any given place and I'll give you fifty-fifty odds, someone is fucking up. So, when things go up in literal flames, it's generally a safe assumption that, you know...

ALEX: Setting that aside, the question is whether we handled it in the best way we could have.

DARA: Our reputation is only slightly better than Stalin's, so obviously not. (*To Vick*) But if you're right, then it sounds like a no–win. No one wants to hear that sometimes bad things just happen and there's nothing anyone can do to stop it. They want it to be someone's *fault*.

VICK: I don't think issuing statement after statement saying "We don't know anything yet and please stay calm and we'll tell you something, someday, when we know something concrete, which might be never because the fire, oh so conveniently, may have destroyed all the evidence," did much good for anyone.

ALEX: Sometimes people just want to be angry. (*Beat*) And we still don't know that they're wrong to be – that's being investigated.

DARA: So what? Fine, people want a simple story where it's easy to tell who's to blame and it will never happen again because we'll get rid of *those* people and then we'll all sleep easier knowing they've been cast into the outer darkness, but... People want a lot of things that are bad for them. It doesn't mean we hand them the crystal meth and say "go ahead, have a smoke."

SAM: And you think, what, our slant on the story should be "Shit happens for no reason and if you find the idea that you live in an indifferent universe completely terrifying, well that's tough titty for you?" It might not be the winning strategy you imagine.

DARA: I'm not saying that – I'm saying, if people are invested in the idea that institutions don't care when they get hurt, or even that we want to hurt them, and the press are going to default to telling *that* story anyway, because it's simple and it doesn't require thought and it gets people good and angry so they'll click on things... I don't see a way out. People will cling onto things that make them feel safe when they're scared, even if they don't make sense, so... our cold hard dose of fact was never going to be as attractive as that story. Once you know who's to blame, you think

	you know what has to be fixed so that it never happens again.
VICK:	You've forgotten, most of the time… most of the time, that story is true. Or at least true enough for a thirty second spot on the news – which is as true as it needs to be. You can't blame people for drawing the obvious conclusions when there's no other convincing explanation, especially when as far as they know they get lied to all the time.
DARA:	You were just saying that the truth isn't what they want to hear, so –
ALEX:	We've strayed a little. About the families.
DARA:	*We* couldn't contact them. If the first people who get in touch are the press office, all "sorry for your tragic loss and also please don't say anything bad about us in public"…it's just more proof that the only thing we care about is how we look, not the people who worked for us and got nicely seared in the fire, and *I* don't fancy making that phone call.
ALEX:	Do you need a minute?

Dara gestures – no, they can continue.

| **SAM:** | I still think someone should have warned them or passed on a number or something. Most journalists are potatoes on legs, no one needs to see that first thing in the morning, let alone after – |

VICK: They send the babies to do the death knocks, so they're usually fairly cute looking. I mean the trainees.

DARA: What?

VICK: Have to toughen them up somehow. Besides, it's not the kind of job you do if you can make someone else do it for you, you know what I mean?

ALEX: So, maybe the Boss should have given them our contact details, in case they wanted to use them, or – it's tricky to avoid that impression though, I know what you mean Dara. Anything else?

VICK: We should have done an interview the next day.

DARA: This again? The fire hadn't even gone out yet, we didn't know what we were dealing with.

VICK: But we could have said even that much in person, rather than –

ALEX: The Boss had maybe two hours sleep, and then spent the morning talking to the families, that's not good preparation for an interview.

DARA: Would they even have let us do an interview like that as a pre–record? Because live seems like multiple, many serious risks.

VICK: I'm sure he can talk live for a hundred and fifty seconds without making an idiot of himself.

ALEX: And I think you may be the press office's official optimist. If it was that easy none of us would have jobs. (*Beat*) Have you ever listened to the Boss talk?

DARA: One wrong answer – one second where the audience thinks a question's being dodged and suddenly we don't just *seem* evil, everyone *knows* we're evil, because we've confirmed it. "Look at that heartless bastard who can barely get a sympathetic sentence out, let alone look like a human being for thirty whole seconds." We'd have proved everyone right.

VICK: Saying nothing is still a message. It had the exact same effect in the end, and you know it.

ALEX: So, it sounds like media training for the Boss would be a good idea, is what I'm getting from this, ideally *before* the next disaster. And then if we do have to make that decision, we can do it with confidence that the interview is something we can actually manage, instead of being terrified at the mere thought. Anything else?

DARA: We need a grab bag – something that's ready to go if we ever have another disaster. We weren't evacuated, but the two other buildings were, and we could have wound up running the press response from inside the evacuation. I don't like the idea of having to go mobile with a battery that's running down.

SAM: Would have given us an excuse not to answer.

VICK: More importantly, we needed them to make someone tell us what the hell was going on, sooner than the day *after* the accident. If we'd been able to say "the explosion happened because of thing X" that would have shut down a lot of the speculation. We were getting calls from people who knew more than we did

DARA: Not helped by the fact that some of our own people were merrily suggesting every bad thing they could think of on twitter.

ALEX: Look, you can't blame people for being... unwise in a bad situation.

DARA: Yes I can.

ALEX: You're right, that was silly of me. (*Beat*) It's something we're going to talk about. But look, despite how all this sounds... everyone knows how difficult it was. We were under an unbelievable amount of pressure, we're not used to it, and... And if you need time off to rest and recover or... anything else, just... let me know. I've got to take all of this to the meeting, so... thanks.

Alex leaves, taking Sam's notes

VICK: So, think we need to start drafting a resignation?

DARA: We wait to do that until Alex tells us – if the Boss were to find out...

SAM: How about a doughnut instead?

DARA: With all of my heart, never again.

VICK: You really don't want anything that reminds you of that week, do you?

SAM: Are you quitting bananas too?

DARA: For now at least. They make me feel sick.

SCENE SIX

Four months later – the office. It's the Christmas party, but a cheap one.

Vick enters, pauses to check for messages.

Dara follows a moment later.

DARA: You're not leaving

VICK: Well –

DARA: I know Sam was waffling on about how we stepped up to the crisis and bravely saved our reputation in the eyes of the world or whatever... but don't let it get to you. It's not meant to –

VICK: It's meant to make Sam seem impressive and brilliant and interesting to anyone listening, I worked that part out. Kind of bad form though, given the occasion, don't you think?

DARA: It's not meant to get to you, that's all I was saying.

VICK: I know that.

DARA: And yet. I had no idea so many things happened that day, but to hear that story it... we all laughed more than a clown at a wake.

VICK: You're the one who doesn't like it. You only came running out after me so you'd have an excuse to leave.

DARA: That's not the only reason.

VICK: But it is.

Pause

DARA: I hate when Sam talks about it like... like it was a good day for us. I mean, I know that's not what's *meant*, it's just how it sounds, all these funny stories about... you'd think it was entertaining.

VICK: It was a little funny.

DARA: We must remember that day very differently, because... there isn't a single bright spot in my –

VICK: Not a single one?

DARA: (*Pause*) That was after.

VICK: No, it was part of it – it was because of it. You wouldn't have accepted that I'm a person you like anywhere near as fast if –

DARA: I never said that.

VICK: No. You didn't say it. But you stopped staring at me like you were trying to come up with five different plans to make me quit and then maybe sell my kidneys.

DARA: Those were only options. I was still working on my cunning plan to drive you away.

VICK: Anyway – I reached the obvious conclusion.

DARA: (*Beat*) You know what the Boss is doing with his early retirement? He's adopted one of the cats.

VICK: The ginger?

DARA: How did you know?

VICK: The ginger was my favourite.

DARA: Of course she was.

Pause

VICK: It's the poor saps they sent out to do the death knocks I feel sorry for.

DARA: Why?

VICK: Because I've done it.

DARA: Seriously?

VICK: More than once. (*Beat*) It's not a perk of the job, but –

DARA: Well I'd hope not. Trampling all over a grieving family isn't –

VICK: It's not always terrible.

DARA: Yes, and even cancer has its upsides.

VICK: Sometimes – okay, mostly it's terrible, but sometimes… sometimes you get to… help someone find out why this catastrophic thing has happened to them, when no one will tell them anything, when they're stumbling around, bewildered, because the floor of their life just fell in and everyone says it's too soon to say anything conclusive on the question of building collapses.

DARA: You give them someone to blame, is what you mean.

VICK: It helps people find their feet if they can at least tell themselves they know why. When your entire life falls apart that way... it's like gravity has stopped working, but only for you.

DARA: (*Pause*) Why didn't you ever tell me?

VICK: Tell you –

DARA: You knew I was me – you remembered me from the wedding, you knew my full name, even though I didn't know yours, and you called me up however many times a week for nearly two years, and never thought to say 'Remember when?' And you knew – you must have known – that's why you were so –

VICK: I thought we both knew.

DARA: And the fact that I never said – that didn't strike you as odd.

VICK: I thought it – I thought it was between us. A private joke or something.

DARA: So there were years' worth of subtext I had no idea was even happening. (*Beat*) That is a little funny.

VICK: Why?

DARA: Because... obviously.

VICK: Why?

DARA: Was this your usual tactic, interrogate people until they give in and tell you what you want to hear?

VICK: You'd be surprised how often it works. Why?

DARA: Because... if you'd only said something at the start – the first time you called – it wouldn't have taken literally an explosive incident for us to... for us to have said anything real.

VICK: Oh but it might have done.

DARA: Even I'm not that stubborn.

VICK: No?

DARA: No.

Pause

DARA: After, I kept dreaming about phone calls and waking myself up. Too many questions from too many people, and you were another person demanding an answer. (*Beat*) But I liked it. So we're clear. I was just... overwhelmed.

VICK: Are you overwhelmed *now*?

DARA: No.

Kiss

VICK: Did you like that? Tell the truth.

DARA: *You* tell the truth – I've done my fair share of gushing out things I never meant to say tonight, so… what's your slant?

VICK: Oh, you want me to spin it?

DARA: No, I meant… tell me the truth, but intelligently – so I hear what you actually want me to hear instead of… instead of whatever unfair assumption I might make.

VICK: I'm leaving.

Pause

DARA: Not lying, that is not where I expected the conversation to go. The Boss' resignation got to you that much?

VICK: It wasn't his fault. They said so at the inquests.

DARA: But by then no one cared. And maybe it was. At least, enough. Enough for the story.

VICK: Yeah, I'm… not a good fit. For all of this. I don't want to be 'intelligent,' I don't want to slant everything I say. I'm much better at just explaining why.

DARA: So, back to press then? Secure employment not something you feel the need of in the twenty–first century?

VICK: It's broadcast this time, radio, and a different subject – so, I won't be calling you up and annoying you anymore.

DARA: Oh, okay.

VICK: At least, not for work reasons.

DARA: Right.

VICK: So, the next time Sam is boring someone's ear off about the day the crisis happened, you can say it's how we... reconciled.

DARA: But that's not true.

VICK: It's true enough. And it makes for a good story, so it might as well be.

END